Contents

Meeting Special Needs of Children

AIMS OF THE PROGRAM

In any class, one or more students may be unable to play and perform basic motor skills effectively. If these students can't play, run, jump, and throw at an early age, they may be slow to develop essential motor skills as well as other basic learnings and social skills—or not develop them at all.

Play is a child's way of learning and integrating skills that will be used throughout life. Through play, children come to understand the world about them. Through play, children learn to move and move to learn. And as children gain play and motor skills, their feelings of self-worth and their positive self-images grow.

Most children learn to play and move through the activities of childhood. They learn by interacting with the environment and with their brothers and sisters and their peers. Handicapped children and other children with special needs often lack the opportunities to play with their peers. These children do not develop play and motor skills on their own. They need a structured, sequential curriculum to interact with their peers, gain feelings of self-worth, and achieve success—and the sooner these children can begin such a program, the better.

This Play and Motor Skills Activities Series presents a program of effective instruction strategies through which all children can achieve success in the general physical education program. It is not a pull-out program (that is, the child is not pulled out for therapy or special tutorial assistance); it is not a fix-it program (that is, the child is not segregated until all deficits are remediated). It is a positive program for each child to succeed in a play-and-motor-skills activity program. It is designed to help you, the teacher, set up sequential curricula, plan each child's instructional program, and teach effectively so that each child progresses toward desired learning outcomes.

Three Major Aims of the Program

1. To enable each child to perform basic play and motor skills at the level of his or her abilities;

2. To help each child use these skills in play and daily living activities to maximize his or her health, growth, and development, as well as joy in movement; and

3. To enhance each child's feelings of self-worth and self-confidence as a learner while moving to learn and learning to move.

BOOKS IN THE SERIES

There are eight books in this Play and Motor Skills Activities Series for preprimary through early primary grades, ages 3–7 years.

1. Locomotor Activities
2. Ball-Handling Activities
3. Stunts and Tumbling Activities
4. Health and Fitness Activities
5. Rhythmic Activities
6. Body Management Activities
7. Play Activities
8. Planning for Teaching

The seven activities books are designed to help teachers of children with handicaps and other special-needs children. Each book provides sequential curricula by skill levels. Each book is complete within its cover: sequential skills and teaching activities, games, action words, and checklists for the class's record of progress in each skill and an Individual Record of Progress (IRP) report.

Book 8, *Planning for Teaching,* is an essential companion to each of the seven activities books because it presents not only the steps for planning a teaching unit and providing for individual differences in each lesson, but it also includes a guide to incorporating social skills into units and lessons and also outlines a Home Activities Program. These two guides are particularly important for children with special needs. Because they often have limited opportunities to interact with their peers, these children need planned, sequential learning experiences to develop socially acceptable behaviors. And because special-needs children also often need extensive practice to retain a skill and generalize its use, a Home Activities Program, planned jointly by parents and teacher, can give them the necessary additional structured learning opportunities.

SEQUENTIAL CURRICULA: SUCCESS BY LEVELS

Each child and the teacher evaluate success. Success is built into the sequential curricula by levels of skills and teaching activities.

Each skill is divided into three levels: rudimentary Skill Level 1 and more refined Skill Levels 2 and 3. Each level is stated in observable behavioral movement terms. The skill levels become performance objectives. Children enter the sequential program at their own performance levels. As they add one small success to another and gain a new skill component or move to a higher skill level, they learn to listen, follow directions, practice, create, and play with others.

Within each skill level, your activities are sequenced, so the child can gain understanding progressively. Within each skill, you provide cues to meet each child's level of understanding and ability. The continuum of teaching cues is

1. verbal cues (action words) with physical assistance or prompts throughout the movement,

2. verbal cues and demonstrations,

3. verbal challenges and problem-solving cues such as "can you?" and

4. introduction of self-initiated learning activities.

GAMES

Game activities are identified for each performance objective by skill level in the seven activity books. At the end of each activity book is an alphabetized description of the games. This list includes the name of each game, formation, directions, equipment, skills involved in playing, and the type of play. Just before the list, you'll find selection criteria and ways to adapt games to different skill levels. Many of the game activities can be used to teach several objectives.

ACTION WORDS

Words for actions (step, look, catch, kick), objects (foot, ball, hand), and concepts (slow, fast, far) are used as verbal cues in teaching. These action words should be matched to the child's level of understanding. They provide a bridge to connect skill activities with other classroom learnings. In the seven activity books, action words are identified for each performance objective by skill level, and an alphabetized list of Action Words is provided at the beginning of each book. As you use this program, add words that are used in other classroom activities and delete those that the children are not ready to understand.

CHECKLISTS:
A CHILD'S RECORD OF PROGRESS

In each activity book, you'll also find Individual and Class Records of Progress listing each performance objective. You can use one or both to record the entry performance level and progress of each child. The child's Individual Record of Progress can be used as part of the Individualized Educational Program (IEP). The teacher can record the child's entry performance level and progress on the child's IEP report form or use the end-of-the-year checklist report.

By observing each child performing the skills in class (e.g., during play, during teaching of the skill or in set-aside time), you can meet the special needs of each child. By using the checklists to record each child's entry level performance of objectives to be taught, you can develop an instructional plan for and evaluate the progress of each child.

Assign each child a learning task (skill component or skill level) based on lesson objectives, and plan lesson activities based on the entry performance level to help the child achieve success. Then use the checklists to record, evaluate, and report each child's progress to the parents. With this record of progress, you can review the teaching-learning activities and can make changes to improve them as necessary.

TEACHING STRATEGY
Direct Instruction

Direct Instruction is coaching on specific tasks at a skill level that allows each child to succeed. A structured and sequential curriculum of essential skills is the primary component of Direct Instruction. As the child progresses in learning, the teacher poses verbal challenges and problem-solving questions such as "can you?" and "show me!" Direct Instruction is based on the premise that success builds success and failure breeds failure.

Adaptive Instruction

Adaptive Instruction is modifying what is taught and how it is taught in order to respond to each child's special needs. Adaptive Instruction helps teachers become more responsive to individual needs. Teaching is based on the child's abilities, on what is to be taught in the lesson, and on what the child is to achieve at the end of instruction. Lesson plans are based on the child's entry performance level on the skills to be taught. Students are monitored during instruction, and the activities are adjusted to each student's needs. Positive reinforcement is provided, and ways to correct the performance or behavior are immediately demonstrated.

Children enter the curriculum at different skill levels, and they learn at different rates. The sequential curriculum helps teachers to individualize the instruction for each child in the class. Thus, the same skill can be taught in a class that includes Betty, who enters at Skill Level 1, and James, who enters at Skill Level 3, because the activities are prescribed for the class or group, but the lesson is planned in order to focus on each child's learning task, and each child is working to achieve his or her own learning task. What is important is that each child master the essential skills at a level of performance that matches his or her abilities, interests, and joy.

Since children learn skills at different rates, you might want to use the following time estimates to allot instructional time for a child to make meaningful progress toward the desired level of performance. One or two skill components can usually be mastered in the instructional time available.

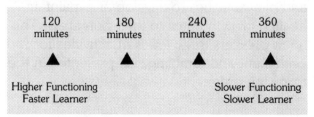

Stunts and Tumbling Skills and Activities

INTRODUCTION

Goals for Each Child

1. To demonstrate the ability to perform basic stunts and tumbling skills taught in the instructional program;

2. To use stunts and tumbling skills in daily living activities in order to maximize healthy development and joy in movement; and

3. To gain greater feelings of self-worth and self-confidence and to gain greater ability in moving to learn and learning to move.

Stunts and tumbling activities are an important part of children's overall movement experiences. These activities provide opportunities to learn how to control body movements in a variety of situations and to learn directional concepts of right and left, near and far, up and down, and forward and backward. Strength, flexibility, and endurance are all important aspects of these activities. Stunts and tumbling skills require "controlled" movements rather than speed. They are introduced in early childhood and preschool years as part of a program of exploratory and creative movement learning experiences.

Children with special needs in preschool through early elementary years require planned, structured, and sequenced motor and play activities to develop and maintain healthy growth equal to their potentials. This book presents three levels of activities for each stunt and tumbling skill presented in the following order:

1. Log Roll
2. Forward Roll
3. Backward Roll
4. Static Balancing
5. Dynamic Balancing
6. Parachute

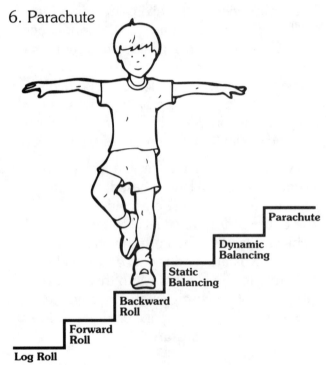

GETTING STARTED

To begin, decide which stunts and tumbling skills you will teach. You can plan a unit or a week or a day or a year. You may decide to teach all skills in this book. Or you may select just a few. Review the checklist for each skill objective you select to teach. Become familiar with the skill components. Next, decide which action words and games you will use in teaching these skills.

Action Words

The words you use are teaching cues. Select ones your children will understand. For each of the stunts and tumbling skills, action words are listed by skill level, and an alphabetized list of words for all the skills in this book is provided below. Circle the words you will use in teaching. If the words you selected prove too difficult for your students, cross them out. Add others that are more appropriate for your children. Star those words that work well.

ACTION	OBJECT	CONCEPT
Balance	Arm	Across
Bend	Back	Back
Extend	Balance beam	Backward
Go	Balance board	Between
Grasp	Balls	Center
Hold	Barrel	Down
Kneel	Beanbag	Fast
Land	Blanket	Forward
Lift	Boards	Front
Move	Chair	Look
Pull	Chin	Middle
Push	Foot	Off
Raise	Footprints	On
Reach	Geometric shapes	Over
Ripple	Hand	Overhead
Roll	Head	Ready
Squat	Knees	Ready position
Stand	Leg	Rear
Step	Lines	Round
Stop	Mat	Show me
Straddle	Mushroom	Side
Tuck	Palms	Straight
Turn	Parachute	Tight
Walk	Picture	Together
	Shoulder	Up
	Toe	Upper
	Toy	
	Umbrella	

Games and Play Activities

For each skill level, you'll find a list of games; select the activity matched to the skills you plan to teach. At the end of this book, you'll find a list of games along with a description of each of them. You'll note that some of the games can be used to teach more than one skill. Use this master list to note those games and play activities that work well and those that do not. Make your comments right on the game listed, or set up a similar format for the games you have selected and make your comments on that sheet. This kind of information can help you plan successful teaching activities.

Equipment

One or more of the following pieces of equipment will be needed for most of the stunts and tumbling games:

1. Whistle for signals
2. Mats or pads for landing
3. Balance beams
4. Balance boards
5. Drum, tambourine, record player
6. Toys
7. Barrels
8. Blankets
9. Traffic cones
10. Colored tape or chalk
11. Ladders
12. Colored cutout shapes
13. Beanbags, geometric shapes
14. Parachute
15. Balls of various sizes and weights

Space

Stunts and tumbling activities require enough space for children to perform the skills comfortably and safely. The size of the space depends on the equipment available for the activities and games selected and on the number of children in the class. A multipurpose room and a playground are desirable.

Health and Safety

Space and the equipment should be arranged for safety (mats for rolls and balance beams and boards with chairs alongside for balancing activities). Children with braces, crutches, or wheelchairs may need assistance with rolling activities on mats. You will need to determine the safety of balancing activities for children with orthopedic impairments. Children with special visual needs may need a tour of the space and equipment (mats, boards, beams) before the lesson. A buddy can be assigned to be near the child when the lesson is taught. Children with special hearing needs may need to be close to the teacher or leader of the activity. The teacher should be positioned to observe all the children during the lesson activities.

Organization: Learning Centers

Learning centers are one of the best types of class organization. You can plan small group learning centers when you know each child's level of performance of the stunt or tumbling activity to be taught. Learning centers can be used to group children by levels of ability or to mix children of different levels of ability. The number of learning centers and their purpose will depend on the number of teachers and support personnel: aides, parent volunteers, older peer models.

To set up a learning center, you should consider the following:

1. Purpose	Skills to be taught and practiced
2. Levels	Levels 1, 2, and 3, or only one, determined by size of class, space, equipment, support personnel
3. Grouping	Same or mixed skill levels
4. Physical setting	Location, such as playground or multipurpose room; equipment available; existing physical boundaries, such as walls, or space to make boundaries with chairs, benches, mats, tapes
5. Activities	Type of game or instructional activity such as running on paths, jumping over lines, climbing jungle gym

LEARNING CENTERS: STUNTS AND TUMBLING ACTIVITIES

LEARNING CENTER 1

Location: Gymnasium

Skill: Forward and backward roll

Activity: Roll forward on incline, roll backward on mat, log roll on mattress

Grouping: Children at same or different skill levels

LEARNING CENTER 2

Location: Park playground

Skill: Dynamic balancing

Activity: Balance around sandbox, on log, on tires, on inclined boards

Grouping: Children at same or different skill levels

LEARNING CENTER 3

Location: School playground

Skill: Parachute

Activity: Run around with the parachute and play games using it

Grouping: Children at same or different skill levels

Stunts and Tumbling Activities

LOG ROLL: SKILL LEVEL 1

Performance Objective

The child with ability to assume a front lying position with arms extended overhead and legs together can perform a log roll three consecutive times, demonstrating the following skill components:

On an 8-foot mat, the child can

1. roll from front to back, keeping arms extended overhead and legs together, and

2. roll from back to front, keeping arms extended overhead and legs together.

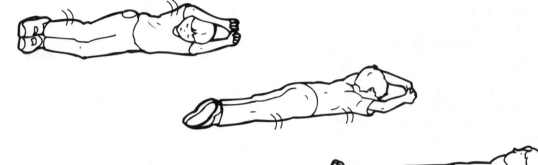

Action Words

Actions: Extend, go, move, roll, stop, turn

Objects: Arm, barrel, blanket, head, leg, mat, picture, toy

Concepts: Back, front, look, overhead, ready, show me, side, straight, together

Games

- Did You Ever See a Lassie/Laddie?
- Do What I Do
- Follow the Leader
- Obstacle Course
- Roll and Toss
- Roll Away
- Roll Like a Ball
- Rolling Down Grassy Hills
- Rolling in Snow to Make Body Prints
- Rolling Into/Out of a Blanket
- Rolling Races

TEACHING ACTIVITIES

If a child requires assistance to respond,

1. give verbal cues and physical assistance. Manipulate or guide the child through the entire skill. Place the child on back with arms and legs extended. Turn the child's head to the side, and assist the child in turning shoulder and hip one-half turn in the same direction. Give the child specific verbal instructions throughout (in sign language, bliss symbols, action cues), such as "Get to the mat," "Lie down and roll," "Ready, go."

2. give verbal cues with demonstration. Use a model or have the child watch you roll from back to side and vice versa. Then have the child perform the action. Use specific verbal instructions (as in 1 above with the modeling).

If a child can respond without assistance,

3. give a verbal challenge in the form of a problem: "Who can . . . ?" "Show me how you can . . ."

a. Roll onto the mat while I pull the blanket underneath you.
b. Roll down the mat incline to the bottom.
c. Roll along the colored tape on the mat.
d. Roll onto the body silhouette on the mat.
e. Variation: Roll to music (drum).

4. introduce self-initiated learning activities.
Set up the equipment (mats) and space for rolling. Provide time at the beginning of the lesson and free time for independent learning after the child understands the skills to be used. You may ask the child to create a game activity to play alone or with others (partner or small group) on and around the equipment.

5. Variations: Set up an obstacle course that includes colored tape, obstacles (mats, inclines) to roll on. Play a game, such as Roll Away, Rolling on the Grassy Hills, or Follow the Leader, that incorporates rolling activities.

LOG ROLL: SKILL LEVEL 2

Performance Objective

The child with acquisition of Skill Level 1 can perform a log roll three consecutive times, demonstrating the following skill components:

On a 10-foot mat, the child can

3. roll from front to back to front with arms extended overhead and legs together and

4. roll from back to front to back with arms extended overhead and legs together.

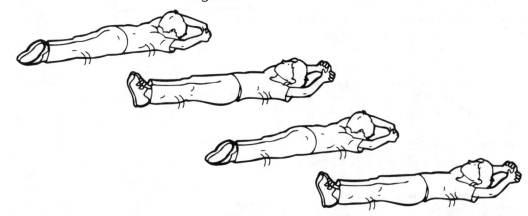

Skills to Review

1. Roll from front to back, keeping arms extended overhead and legs together, and

2. roll from back to front, keeping arms extended overhead and legs together.

Action Words

Actions: Extend, go, move, roll, stop, turn

Objects: Arm, barrel, blanket, head, leg, mat, picture, toy

Concepts: Back, front, look, overhead, ready, show me, side, straight, together

Games

- Did You Ever See a Lassie/Laddie?
- Do What I Do
- Follow the Leader
- Obstacle Course
- Roll and Toss
- Roll Away
- Roll Like a Ball
- Rolling Down Grassy Hills
- Rolling in Snow to Make Body Prints
- Rolling Into/Out of a Blanket
- Rolling Races

TEACHING ACTIVITIES

If a child requires assistance to respond,

1. give verbal cues and physical assistance.
Manipulate or guide the child through the entire skill. Place the child on back with arms and legs extended. Turn the child's head to the side, and assist the child in turning shoulder and hip one-half turn in the same direction (from front to back) and then again from back to front one-half turn. Give the child specific verbal instructions throughout (in sign language, bliss symbols, action cues), such as "Get to the mat," "Lie down and roll," "Ready, go."

2. give verbal cues with demonstration.
Use a model or have the child watch you roll from back to side and vice versa. Then have the child perform the action. Use specific verbal instructions (as in 1 above with the modeling).

If a child can respond without assistance,

3. give a verbal challenge in the form of a problem: "Who can . . . ?" "Show me how you can . . ."

a. Roll on the mat and move the large cardboard barrel across the floor.

b. Roll down the bar and stay on the line taped down the center of the mat.

c. Roll down the mat and watch the toy at the end of the mat. Get the toy!

d. Roll down grassy slopes.

e. Roll over in the wading pool from front to back float and then front float.

f. Variations: Roll to music (start as music begins, stop as music ends). Roll on different surfaces (mats, carpeting, floor, inclines).

4. introduce self-initiated learning activities. Set up the equipment (mats) and space for rolling. Provide time at the beginning of the lesson and free time for independent learning after the child understands the skills to be used. You may ask the child to create a game activity to play alone or with others (partner or small group) on and around the equipment.

5. Variations: Set up an obstacle course that includes colored tape, obstacles (mats, inclines) to roll on. Play a game, such as Roll Away, Rolling on the Grassy Hills, or Follow the Leader, that incorporates rolling activities.

LOG ROLL: SKILL LEVEL 3

Performance Objective

The child with acquisition of Skill Level 2 or a level of performance appropriate for the child's level of functioning can maintain that level over six weeks.

Given activities that require the skill, the child can

1. play two or more games listed below at home or school, and
2. play with equipment selected by teacher and parent(s).

Skills to Review

1. Level 1 log roll. Roll from front to back, keeping arms extended overhead and legs together, and
2. roll from back to front, keeping arms extended overhead and legs together.
3. Level 2 log roll. Roll from front to back to front with arms extended overhead and legs together and
4. roll from back to front to back with arms extended overhead and legs together.

Action Words

Actions: Extend, go, move, roll, stop, turn

Objects: Arm, barrel, blanket, head, leg, mat, picture, toy

Concepts: Back, front, look, overhead, ready, show me, side, straight, together

Games

- Did You Ever See a Lassie/Laddie?
- Do What I Do
- Follow the Leader
- Obstacle Course
- Roll and Toss
- Roll Away
- Roll Like a Ball
- Rolling Down Grassy Hills
- Rolling in Snow to Make Body Prints
- Rolling Into/Out of a Blanket
- Rolling Races

TEACHING ACTIVITIES FOR MAINTENANCE

In Teaching

1. Provide the child with teaching cues (verbal and nonverbal, such as demonstration, modeling, imitating) for log roll that involve the skill components the child has achieved in compatible teaching and play activities. Bring to the child's attention the skill components he or she has already achieved. Provide positive reinforcement and feedback for the child.

2. Use games that require log rolling and that involve imitating, modeling, and demonstrating.

3. Observe and assess each child's maintenance at the end of two weeks. Repeat at the end of four weeks (if maintained) and six weeks after initial date of attainment.

▲ Box in the skill level to be maintained on the child's Class Record of Progress. Note the date the child attained target level of performance (defined by teacher alone or co-planned with parents).

▲ Two weeks after attainment, observe the child. Is the level maintained? If child does not demonstrate the skill components at the desired level of performance, indicate the skill components that need reteaching or reinforcing in the comments sheet on the Class Record of Progress. Reschedule teaching time, and co-plan with parents the home activities necessary to reinforce child's achievement of the skill components and maintenance of attainment.

▲ Continue to observe the child, and reteach and reinforce until the child maintains that level of performance for six weeks.

▲ Plan teaching activities incorporating these components so that the child can continually use and reinforce them and can acquire new ones over the year.

▲ When the child can understand it, make a checklist poster illustrating the child's achievements. Bring the child's attention to these skill components in various compatible play and game activities throughout the year. Have the child help others—a partner or a small group.

In Co-Planning with Parent(s)

1. Encourage the parent(s) to reinforce the child's achievement of the skill components in everyday play and living activities in the home.

▲ Provide key action words for the parent(s) to emphasize.

▲ Give the parent(s) a list of play and games to use in playing with the child, thus reinforcing the skill components the child has achieved and needs support to maintain.

▲ Give the parent(s) a list of rolling activities that can be done at home with the child, such as

   a. Rolling away from all your friends as fast as you can.

   b. Rolling into and out of the blanket on the mat. See how fast you can do it.

   c. Rolling down the grassy slope and seeing who can reach the bottom first.

   d. Rolling in the snow and making your body prints in the snow.

   e. Variation: Rolling to music (starting and stopping with music).

2. Set up a time every two weeks to interact with the parent(s) and exchange feedback on the child's progress.

FORWARD ROLL: SKILL LEVEL 1

Performance Objective

The child with ability to do a log roll in a tight tuck position can perform a forward roll three consecutive times, demonstrating the following skill components:

On an 8-foot mat, the child can

1. kneel or squat with hands on mat near head, palms down, and
2. tuck chin down to chest, round back, hold knees slightly apart and close to chin, and then
3. roll across back to sitting position in two or more rolls.

Action Words

Actions: Bend, land, lift, roll, squat, stand, tuck

Objects: Arm, back, chin, hands, knees, leg, mat

Concepts: Across, back, forward, look, ready, show me, up, upper

Games

- Did You Ever See a Lassie/Laddie?
- Do What I Do
- Follow the Leader
- Obstacle Course
- Roll and Toss
- Roll Away
- Roll Like a Ball
- Rolling Down Grassy Hills
- Rolling in Snow to Make Body Prints
- Rolling Into/Out of a Blanket
- Rolling Races

TEACHING ACTIVITIES

If a child requires assistance to respond,

1. give verbal cues and physical assistance.
Manipulate or guide the child through the entire skill. Have child stand on mat with feet together. Manipulate the child into squat with hands flat on the mat. Knees should be bent but not touching mat. Put your hand on the child's back or neck to tuck chin to chest. Keep one hand on the child's head and the other on back of thighs. Lift the child's hips and keep tucking as he or she rolls on back. Give the child specific verbal instructions throughout (in sign language, bliss symbols, action cues), such as "Stand on the mat, squat down," "Put hands flat on mat," "Tuck your head," "Roll over."

2. give verbal cues with demonstration.
Use a model or have the child watch you perform a forward roll by squatting with hands and feet on mat and, chin tucked, rolling forward, pushing with hands, and rolling across back to your feet. Then have the child perform the action. Use specific verbal instructions (as in 1 above with the modeling).

If a child can respond without assistance,

3. **give a verbal challenge in the form of a problem: "Who can . . . ?" "Show me how you can . . ."**

   a. Roll forward down the mat with your chin touching the tape on your chest.

   b. Make yourself into a ball and roll forward. Roll forward down the incline mat.

   c. Variations: Roll down the mat putting your hands on the footprints. Roll to music.

4. **introduce self-initiated learning activities.**
Set up the equipment (mats) and space for rolling. Provide time at the beginning of the lesson and free time for independent learning after the child understands the skills to be used. You may ask the child to create a game activity to play alone or with others (partner or small group) on and around the equipment.

5. **Variations:** Set up an obstacle course that includes colored tape, obstacles (mats, inclines) to roll on. Play a game, such as Roll Away or Rolling Like a Ball, that incorporates rolling activities.

Performance Objective

The child with acquisition of Skill Level 1 can perform a forward roll three consecutive times, demonstrating the following skill components:

On a 10-foot mat, the child can

4. push with hands, palms down on the mat and roll forward in tight tuck position to sitting or standing position.

Skills to Review

1. Kneel or squat with hands on mat near head, palms down, and
2. tuck chin down near chest, round back, hold knees slightly apart and close to chin, and then
3. roll forward across back to sitting position in two or more rolls.

Action Words

Actions: Bend, land, lift, roll, squat, stand, tuck

Objects: Arm, back, chin, hands, knees, leg, mat

Concepts: Across, back, forward, look, ready, show me, up, upper

Games

- Did You Ever See a Lassie/Laddie?
- Do What I Do
- Follow the Leader
- Obstacle Course
- Roll and Toss
- Roll Away
- Roll Like a Ball
- Rolling Down Grassy Hills
- Rolling in Snow to Make Body Prints
- Rolling Into/Out of a Blanket
- Rolling Races

TEACHING ACTIVITIES

If a child requires assistance to respond,

1. give verbal cues and physical assistance.
Manipulate or guide the child through the entire skill. Have child stand on mat with feet together. Manipulate the child into squat with hands flat on the mat. Knees should be bent but not touching mat. Put your hand on the child's back or neck to tuck chin to chest. Keep one hand on the child's head and the other on back of thighs. Lift the child's hips and keep tucking as he or she rolls on back. Make sure child lands on back of neck and upper back. Manipulate the child onto feet in a tuck position. Give the child specific verbal instructions throughout (in sign language, bliss symbols, action cues), such as "Stand on the mat, squat down," "Put hands flat on mat," "Tuck your head," "Roll over."

2. give verbal cues with demonstration.
Use a model or have the child watch you perform a forward roll by squatting with hands and feet on mat and, chin tucked, rolling forward, pushing with hands, and rolling across back to your feet. Then have the child perform the action. Use specific verbal instructions (as in 1 above with the modeling).

If a child can respond without assistance,

3. **give a verbal challenge in the form of a problem: "Who can . . . ?" "Show me how you can . . ."**

   a. Roll forward down the mat on the line. Roll straight.

   b. Roll forward on the X's down the mat.

   c. Roll forward down the incline mat; land on your feet.

   d. Variations: Roll to music, roll on various surfaces (grass, snow, mats, mattress).

4. **introduce self-initiated learning activities.** Set up the equipment (mats) and space for rolling. Provide time at the beginning of the lesson and free time for independent learning after the child understands the skills to be used. You may ask the child to create a game activity to play alone or with others (partner or small group) on and around the equipment.

5. **Variations:** Set up an obstacle course that includes colored tape, obstacles (mats, inclines) to roll on. Play a game, such as Roll Away or Rolling Like a Ball, that incorporates rolling activities.

FORWARD ROLL: SKILL LEVEL 3

Performance Objective

The child with acquisition of Skill Level 2 or a level of performance appropriate for the child's level of functioning can maintain that level over six weeks.

Given activities that require the skill, the child can

1. play two or more games listed below at home or school, and
2. play with equipment selected by teacher and parent(s).

Skills to Review

1. Level 1 forward roll. Kneel or squat with hands on mat near head, palms down, and
2. tuck chin down near chest, round back, holding knees slightly apart and close to chin, and then
3. roll forward across back to sitting position in two or more rolls.
4. Level 2 forward roll. Push with hands, palms down on mat, and roll forward in tight tuck position to sitting or standing position.

Action Words

Actions: Bend, land, lift, roll, squat, stand, tuck

Objects: Arm, back, chin, hands, knees, leg, mat

Concepts: Across, back, forward, look, ready, show me, up, upper

Games

- Did You Ever See a Lassie/Laddie?
- Do What I Do
- Follow the Leader
- Obstacle Course
- Roll and Toss
- Roll Away
- Roll Like a Ball
- Rolling Down Grassy Hills
- Rolling in Snow to Make Body Prints
- Rolling Into/Out of a Blanket
- Rolling Races

TEACHING ACTIVITIES FOR MAINTENANCE

In Teaching

1. Provide the child with teaching cues (verbal and nonverbal, such as demonstration, modeling, imitating) for forward roll that involve the skill components the child has achieved in compatible teaching and play activities. Bring to the child's attention the skill components he or she has already achieved. Provide positive reinforcement and feedback for the child.

2. Use games that require forward rolling and that involve imitating, modeling, and demonstrating.

3. Observe and assess each child's maintenance at the end of two weeks. Repeat at the end of four weeks (if maintained) and six weeks after initial date of attainment.

▲ Box in the skill level to be maintained on the child's Class Record of Progress. Note the date the child attained target level of performance (defined by teacher alone or co-planned with parents).

▲ Two weeks after attainment, observe the child. Is the level maintained? If child does not demonstrate the skill components at the desired level of performance, indicate the skill components that need reteaching or reinforcing in the comments sheet on the Class Record of Progress. Reschedule teaching time, and co-plan with parents the home activities necessary to reinforce child's achievement of the skill components and maintenance of attainment.

▲ Continue to observe the child, and reteach and reinforce until the child maintains that level of performance for six weeks.

▲ Plan teaching activities incorporating these components so that the child can continually use and reinforce them and can acquire new ones over the year.

▲ When the child can understand it, make a checklist poster illustrating the child's achievements. Bring the child's attention to these skill components in various compatible play and game activities throughout the year. Have the child help others—a partner or a small group.

In Co-Planning with Parent(s)

1. Encourage the parent(s) to reinforce the child's achievement of the skill components in everyday play and living activities in the home.

▲ Provide key action words for the parent(s) to emphasize.

▲ Give the parent(s) a list of play and games to use in playing with the child, thus reinforcing the skill components the child has achieved and needs support to maintain.

▲ Give the parent(s) a list of rolling activities that can be done at home with the child, such as
   a. Rolling forward down the hill, touching the tree, and running back up the hill.
   b. Rolling forward with the ball to the trash can and throwing the ball in.
   c. Rolling forward like a ball across the carpet to the wall and rolling back again.
   d. Rolling forward in the snow. Don't get your face wet!
   e. Variations: Rolling to music.

2. Set up a time every two weeks to interact with the parent(s) and exchange feedback on the child's progress.

BACKWARD ROLL: SKILL LEVEL 1

Performance Objective

The child with ability to do a forward roll can perform a backward roll three consecutive times, demonstrating the following skill components:

On an 8-foot mat, the child can

1. sit down, close to heels, knees slightly apart and close to chin, hands with palms up, and roll backward and,
2. keeping tight tuck position (chin tucked in, back rounded, knees close to chin), roll across mat with palms on mat, thumbs near head and then
3. come to sitting position with feet on mat, chin tucked in, arms at sides.

Action Words

Actions: Bend, lift, push, roll, squat, tuck

Objects: Back, foot, hand, mat, palms

Concepts: Backward, down, fast, look, over, ready, round, show me, tight

Games

- Did You Ever See a Lassie/Laddie?
- Do What I Do
- Follow the Leader
- Obstacle Course
- Roll and Toss
- Roll Away
- Roll Like a Ball
- Rolling Down Grassy Hills
- Rolling in Snow to Make Body Prints
- Rolling Into/Out of a Blanket
- Rolling Races

TEACHING ACTIVITIES

If a child requires assistance to respond,

1. give verbal cues and physical assistance.
Manipulate or guide the child through the entire skill. Have child stand on mat. Lower the child's body; sit down. Place one hand on child's upper back and your other hand on the front of child's shins. Roll child onto back. Keep knees in tucked position. Place child's hands with thumbs toward head close to the ears. Push with hands against mat to complete roll. Give the child specific verbal instructions throughout (in sign language, bliss symbols, action cues), such as "Squat down on the mat, roll onto your back," "Keep knees close to chin," "Roll onto your shoulders," "Keep rolling," "Push with hands against the mat."

2. give verbal cues with demonstration.
Use a model or have the child watch you perform a backward roll by squatting with hands and feet on mat, pushing with hands and feet to roll backward. Roll in tight tuck position. Land with feet on mat and sit. Then have the child perform the action. Use specific verbal instructions (as in 1 above with the modeling).

If a child can respond without assistance,

3. **give a verbal challenge in the form of a problem: "Who can . . . ?" "Show me how you can . . ."**
   a. Perform a back roll (crouch position) with hands and knees resting on floor (roll backward, bring knees to chest and clasp them with arms). Roll back and forth rhythmically.
   b. Roll backward down the mat.
   c. Curl into a ball and roll backward.
   d. Roll backward down the incline mat.
   e. Variation: Roll to music.

4. **introduce self-initiated learning activities.**
   Set up the equipment (mats) and space for rolling. Provide time at the beginning of the lesson and free time for independent learning after the child understands the skills to be used. You may ask the child to create a game activity to play alone or with others (partner or small group) on and around the equipment.

5. **Variations:** Set up an obstacle course that includes colored tape, obstacles (mats, inclines) to roll on. Play a game, such as Roll Away, Rolling on Grassy Hills, Follow the Leader, or Roll and Toss, that incorporates rolling activities.

BACKWARD ROLL: SKILL LEVEL 2

Performance Objective

The child with acquisition of Skill Level 1 can perform a backward roll three consecutive times, demonstrating the following skill components:

On an 8-foot mat, the child can

4. with palms on mat and thumbs toward head, push against mat to complete the roll (backward momentum), body in tight tuck position, and

5. land on feet and stand, maintaining balance, or make two or more continuous rolls.

Skills to Review

1. Sit down, close to heels, knees slightly apart and close to chin, hands with palms up, and roll backward and,

2. keeping body in tight tuck position (chin tucked, back rounded, knees close to chin), roll across mat, palms on mat, thumbs near head, and

3. come to sitting position with feet on mat, arms at sides, chin tucked in.

Action Words

Actions: Bend, lift, push, roll, squat, tuck

Objects: Back, foot, hand, mat, palms

Concepts: Backward, down, fast, look, over, ready, round, show me, tight

Games

- Did You Ever See a Lassie/Laddie?
- Do What I Do
- Follow the Leader
- Obstacle Course
- Roll and Toss
- Roll Away
- Roll Like a Ball
- Rolling Down Grassy Hills
- Rolling in Snow to Make Body Prints
- Rolling Into/Out of a Blanket
- Rolling Races

TEACHING ACTIVITIES

If a child requires assistance to respond,

1. give verbal cues and physical assistance.
Manipulate or guide the child through the entire skill. Have child stand on mat. Lower the child's body, knees bent into squat. Place hands, palms down, on mat. Place one hand on child's upper back and your other hand on the front of child's shins. Roll child onto back. Keep knees in tucked position. Place child's hands with thumbs toward head close to the ears. Push with hands against mat to complete roll. Give the child specific verbal instructions throughout (in sign language, bliss symbols, action cues), such as "Squat down on the mat, roll onto your back," "Keep knees close to chin," "Roll onto your shoulders," "Keep rolling," "Push with hands against the mat."

2. give verbal cues with demonstration.
Use a model or have the child watch you perform a backward roll by squatting with hands and feet on mat, pushing with hands and feet to roll backward. Roll in tight tuck position. Land balanced on feet and stand. Then have the child perform the action. Use specific verbal instructions (as in 1 above with the modeling).

If a child can respond without assistance,

3. give a verbal challenge in the form of a problem: "Who can . . . ?" "Show me how you can . . ."

a. Run to the mat, turn around, perform a backward roll, and run back to the end of your line.

b. Roll backward four times in succession.

c. Roll around the obstacle course and do backward rolls wherever you see mats.

d. Variations: Roll to music. Roll on various surfaces (grass, snow, mats, mattress).

4. introduce self-initiated learning activities.
Set up the equipment (mats) and space for rolling. Provide time at the beginning of the lesson and free time for independent learning after the child understands the skills to be used. You may ask the child to create a game activity to play alone or with others (partner or small group) on and around the equipment.

5. Variations: Set up an obstacle course that includes colored tape, obstacles (mats, inclines) to roll on. Play a game, such as Roll Away, Rolling on Grassy Hills, Follow the Leader, or Roll and Toss, that incorporates rolling activities.

BACKWARD ROLL: SKILL LEVEL 3

Performance Objective

The child with acquisition of Skill Level 2 or a level of performance appropriate for the child's level of functioning can maintain that level over six weeks.

Given activities that require the skill, the child can

1. play two or more games listed below at home or school, and
2. play with equipment selected by teacher and parent(s).

Skills to Review

1. Level 1 backward roll. Sit down, close to heels, knees slightly apart and close to chin, hands with palms up, and roll backward and,
2. keeping body in tight tuck position (chin tucked, back rounded, knees close to chin), roll across mat, palms on mat, thumbs near head, and
3. come to sitting position with feet on mat, arms at sides, chin tucked in.
4. Level 2 backward roll. With palms on mat and thumbs toward head, push against mat to complete the roll (backward momentum), body in tight tuck position and
5. land on feet and stand, maintaining balance, or make two or more continuous rolls.

Action Words

Actions: Bend, lift, push, roll, squat, tuck

Objects: Back, foot, hand, mat, palms

Concepts: Backward, down, fast, look, over, ready, round, show me, tight

Games

- Did You Ever See a Lassie/Laddie?
- Do What I Do
- Follow the Leader
- Obstacle Course
- Roll and Toss
- Roll Away
- Roll Like a Ball
- Rolling Down Grassy Hills
- Rolling in Snow to Make Body Prints
- Rolling Into/Out of a Blanket
- Rolling Races

TEACHING ACTIVITIES FOR MAINTENANCE

In Teaching

1. Provide the child with teaching cues (verbal and nonverbal, such as demonstration, modeling, imitating) for backward roll that involve the skill components the child has achieved in compatible teaching and play activities. Bring to the child's attention the skill components he or she has already achieved. Provide positive reinforcement and feedback for the child.
2. Use games that require backward rolling and that involve imitating, modeling, and demonstrating.
3. Observe and assess each child's maintenance at the end of two weeks. Repeat at the end of four weeks (if maintained) and six weeks after initial date of attainment.

▲ Box in the skill level to be maintained on the child's Class Record of Progress. Note the date the child attained target level of performance (defined by teacher alone or co-planned with parents).

▲ Two weeks after attainment, observe the child. Is the level maintained? If child does not demonstrate the skill components at the desired level of performance, indicate the skill components that need reteaching or reinforcing in the comments sheet on the Class Record of Progress. Reschedule teaching time, and co-plan with parents the home activities necessary to reinforce child's achievement of the skill components and maintenance of attainment.

▲ Continue to observe the child, and reteach and reinforce until the child maintains that level of performance for six weeks.

▲ Plan teaching activities incorporating these components so that the child can continually use and reinforce them and can acquire new ones over the year.

▲ When the child can understand it, make a check-list poster illustrating the child's achievements. Bring the child's attention to these skill components in various compatible play and game activities throughout the year. Have the child help others—a partner or a small group.

In Co-Planning with Parent(s)

1. Encourage the parent(s) to reinforce the child's achievement of the skill components in everyday play and living activities in the home.

▲ Provide key action words for the parent(s) to emphasize.

▲ Give the parent(s) a list of play and games to use in playing with the child, thus reinforcing the skill components the child has achieved and needs support to maintain.

▲ Give the parent(s) a list of rolling activities that can be done at home with the child, such as
   a. Rolling backward down the grassy hills. Be careful where you land.
   b. Rolling backward like a ball around a circle.
   c. Rolling backward as fast as you can to the other fence.
   d. Rolling backward in the snow. What kind of a path do you make?
   e. How else can you roll backward?
   f. Variation: Rolling to music.

2. Set up a time every two weeks to interact with the parent(s) and exchange feedback on the child's progress.

Performance Objective

The child with ability to stand on both feet can perform two-point static balances for five seconds three consecutive times, demonstrating the following skill components:

Within a clear space of 5 feet, the child can

1. stand on a 4-inch line in a forward stride position (toes of rear foot touching heel of front foot), with arms extended out from shoulders and parallel to floor and head up and facing forward;

2. stand on 6-inch-wide board on floor in a forward stride position (toes of rear foot touching heel of front foot), with arms extended out from shoulders and parallel to floor and head up and facing forward; and then

3. stand on 4-inch-wide board on floor in a forward stride position (toes of rear foot touching heel of front foot), with arms extended out from shoulders and parallel to floor and head up and facing forward.

Action Words

Actions: Balance, bend, extend, hold, stand

Objects: Arm, balance board, foot, head, leg, shoulder, toe

Concepts: Forward, front, look, ready, rear, show me, straight

Games

- Balancing Fun
- Did You Ever See a Lassie/Laddie?
- Follow the Leader
- Freeze Balance Tag
- Obstacle Course
- Simon Says
- Static Balance
- Statue in the Garden
- Twister

TEACHING ACTIVITIES

If a child requires assistance to respond,

1. give verbal cues and physical assistance.
Manipulate or guide the child through the entire skill. Place the child on the balance board with feet apart. Holding the child's hands, ask him or her to bend arms and hold them out in front. Give the child specific verbal instructions throughout (in sign language, bliss symbols, action cues), such as "Stand still, bend your knees," "Hold your arms out," "Balance."

2. give verbal cues with demonstration.
Use a model or have the child watch you perform a two-point balance with feet apart, knees bent, and arms out to sides for at least five seconds. Then have the child perform the action. Use specific verbal instructions (as in 1 above with the modeling).

If a child can respond without assistance,

3. give a verbal challenge in the form of a problem: "Who can . . . ?" "Show me how you can . . ."

a. Balance with two feet and two hands on the ground.

b. Balance with one foot and one hand on the ground.

c. Balance with feet together, hands on your waist, on flat piece of 2-inch wood on the ground.

d. Balance on tiptoes with feet together, hands on your waist.

e. Balance on heels, feet together, hands on your waist.

f. Balance on the balance board with arms on your waist.

g. Variation: Balance on board to beat of drum.

4. introduce self-initiated learning activities.
Set up the equipment (mats, balance boards, beams) and space for static balancing. Provide time at the beginning of the lesson and free time for independent learning after the child understands the skills to be used. You may ask the child to create a game activity to play alone or with others (partner or small group) on and around the equipment.

5. Variations: Set up an obstacle course that includes colored tape, obstacles. Play a game, such as Twister, Freeze Balance Tag, or Statues in the Garden, that incorporates static-balancing activities.

STATIC BALANCING: SKILL LEVEL 2

Performance Objective

The child with acquisition of Skill Level 1 can perform one-point static balances for five seconds three consecutive times, demonstrating the following skill components:

Within a clear space of 5 feet, the child can

4. stand on the floor with both feet together, then bend one leg so that lower leg is up and back (bent at a right angle) with arms extended out from shoulders and parallel to the floor and head up and looking forward;

5. stand on the floor with both feet together, then bend one leg so that foot can be placed on the inside of the knee of support leg, with arms extended out from shoulders and parallel to the floor and head up and looking forward; and

6. stand on a 4-inch-wide board or line in a forward stride position (toes of rear foot touching heel of front foot) and bend rear leg up and back at a right angle, with arms extended out from shoulders and parallel to floor and head up and looking forward.

Skills to Review

1. Stand on 4-inch line in a forward stride position (toes of rear foot touching heel of front foot), with arms extended out from shoulders and parallel to floor and head up and facing forward;

2. stand on 6-inch-wide board on floor in a forward stride position (toes of rear foot touching heel of front foot), with arms extended out from shoulders and parallel to floor and head up and facing forward; and then

3. stand on 4-inch-wide board on floor in a forward stride position (toes of rear foot touching heel of front foot), with arms extended out from shoulders and parallel to floor and head up and facing forward.

Action Words

Actions: Balance, bend, extend, hold, stand

Objects: Arm, balance board, foot, head, leg, shoulder, toe

Concepts: Forward, front, look, ready, rear, show me, straight

Games

- Balancing Fun
- Did You Ever See a Lassie/Laddie?
- Follow the Leader
- Freeze Balance Tag
- Obstacle Course
- Simon Says
- Static Balance
- Statue in the Garden
- Twister

TEACHING ACTIVITIES

If a child requires assistance to respond,

1. give verbal cues and physical assistance.
Manipulate or guide the child through the entire skill. While child is standing, extend his or her arms to support weight and lift one leg behind body. Give the child specific verbal instructions throughout (in sign language, bliss symbols, action cues), such as "Pick up your foot," "Stand on one foot," "Hold your other foot out," "Hold your arms out," "Balance."

2. give verbal cues with demonstration.
Use a model or have the child watch you perform a one-point static balance by standing on one foot with arms extended and one leg extended behind you. Balance for five seconds or more. Then have the child perform the action. Use specific verbal instructions (as in 1 above with the modeling).

If a child can respond without assistance,

3. give a verbal challenge in the form of a problem: "Who can . . . ?" "Show me how you can . . ."

a. Balance with one foot on the ground.

b. Balance with one foot on the 2-inch block.

c. Balance with one foot on the mattress.

d. Balance on one foot with your hands on your waist.

e. Balance on one foot with a beanbag on your head.

f. Variations: Balance to music (turned on and off). Balance on different surfaces (grass, sand, cement).

4. introduce self-initiated learning activities.
Set up the equipment (mats, balance boards, beams) and space for static balancing. Provide time at the beginning of the lesson and free time for independent learning after the child understands the skills to be used. You may ask the child to create a game activity to play alone or with others (partner or small group) on and around the equipment.

5. Variations: Set up an obstacle course that includes colored tape, obstacles. Play a game such as Twister, Freeze Balance Tag, or Statue in the Garden, that incorporates static-balancing activities.

STATIC BALANCING: SKILL LEVEL 3

Performance Objective

The child with acquisition of Skill Level 2 or a level of performance appropriate for the child's level of functioning can maintain that level over six weeks.

Given activities that require the skill, the child can

1. play two or more games listed below at home or school, and
2. play with equipment selected by teacher and parent(s).

Skills to Review

1. Level 1 static balancing. Stand on 4-inch line in a forward stride position (toes of rear foot touching heel of front foot), with arms extended out from shoulders and parallel to floor and head up and facing forward;

2. stand on 6-inch-wide board on floor in a forward stride position (toes of rear foot touching heel of front foot), with arms extended out from shoulders and parallel to floor and head up and facing forward; and then

3. stand on 4-inch-wide board on floor in a forward stride position (toes of rear foot touching heel of front foot), with arms extended out from shoulders and parallel to floor and head up and facing forward.

4. Level 2 static balancing. Stand on the floor with both feet together, then bend one leg so that lower leg is up and back (bent at a right angle), with arms extended out from shoulders parallel to floor and head up and looking forward;

5. stand on the floor with both feet together, then bend one leg so that foot can be placed on the inside knee of support leg, with arms extended out from shoulders and parallel to floor and head up and looking forward; and then

6. stand on a 4-inch-wide board or line in a forward stride position (toes or rear foot touching heel of front foot) and bend rear leg up and back, with arms extended out from shoulders and parallel to floor and head up and looking forward.

Action Words

Actions: Balance, bend, extend, hold, stand

Objects: Arm, balance beam, board, foot, head, leg, shoulder, toe

Concepts: Forward, front, look, ready, rear, show me, straight

Games

- Balancing Fun
- Did You Ever See a Lassie/Laddie?
- Follow the Leader
- Freeze Balance Tag
- Obstacle Course Simon Says
- Static Balance
- Statue in the Garden
- Twister

TEACHING ACTIVITIES FOR MAINTENANCE

In Teaching

1. Provide the child with teaching cues (verbal and nonverbal, such as demonstration, modeling, imitating) for static balance that involve the skill components the child has achieved in compatible teaching and play activities. Bring to the child's attention the skill components he or she has already achieved. Provide positive reinforcement and feedback for the child.

2. Use games that require static balancing and that involve imitating, modeling, and demonstrating.

3. Observe and assess each child's maintenance at the end of two weeks. Repeat at the end of four weeks (if maintained) and six weeks after initial date of attainment.

▲ Box in the skill level to be maintained on the child's Class Record of Progress. Note the date the child attained target level of performance (defined by teacher alone or co-planned with parents).

▲ Two weeks after attainment, observe the child. Is the level maintained? If child does not demonstrate the skill components at the desired level of performance, indicate the skill components that need reteaching or reinforcing in the comments sheet on the Class Record of Progress. Reschedule teaching time, and co-plan with parents the home activities necessary to reinforce child's achievement of the skill components and maintenance of attainment.

▲ Continue to observe the child, and reteach and reinforce until the child maintains that level of performance for six weeks.

▲ Plan teaching activities incorporating these components so that the child can continually use and reinforce them and can acquire new ones over the year.

▲ When the child can understand it, make a checklist poster illustrating the child's achievements. Bring the child's attention to these skill components in various compatible play and game activities throughout the year. Have the child help others— a partner or a small group.

In Co-Planning with Parent(s)

1. Encourage the parent(s) to reinforce the child's achievement of the skill components in everyday play and living activities in the home.

▲ Provide key action words for the parent(s) to emphasize.

▲ Give the parent(s) a list of play and games to use in playing with the child, thus reinforcing the skill components the child has achieved and needs support to maintain.

▲ Give the parent(s) a list of static-balancing activities that can be done at home with the child, such as
   a. Standing on log and balancing.
   b. Standing on the balance beam and raising one foot up to balance.
   c. Balancing on a balance board with a beanbag on your head.
   d. Balancing on a teeter-totter.
   e. Holding rocks of unequal weights while balancing on balance board.

2. Set up a time every two weeks to interact with the parent(s) and exchange feedback on the child's progress.

Performance Objective

The child with ability to walk in a controlled manner can walk a 4-inch-wide board placed on the floor three consecutive times, demonstrating the following skill components:

On a balance beam, the child can

1. stand on balance beam on floor and move forward 8 feet in any manner without stepping off board and then

2. alternate feet while walking forward at least six steps without stepping off board.

Action Words

Actions: Go, stand, step, stop, walk

Objects: Beanbag, board, foot, lines

Concepts: Backward, forward, look, off, on, ready, show me, up

Games

- Beanbag Relay
- Did You Ever See a Lassie/Laddie?
- Do What I Do
- Follow the Leader
- Ice Cream Cone Game
- Ladder Game
- Obstacle Course
- Simon Says

TEACHING ACTIVITIES

If a child requires assistance to respond,

1. give verbal cues and physical assistance.
Manipulate or guide the child through the entire skill. Stand behind the child on the board. Walk the child across the board by holding him or her around the waist for support and moving or pushing one foot at a time with your foot. Give the child specific verbal instructions throughout (in sign language, bliss symbols, action cues), such as "Walk across the board," "Look at me."

2. give verbal cues with demonstration.
Use a model or have the child watch you walk across the 4-inch-wide board with your hands extended out at shoulder height. Then have the child perform the action. Use specific verbal instructions (as in 1 above with the modeling).

If a child can respond without assistance,

3. **give a verbal challenge in the form of a problem: "Who can . . . ?" "Show me how you can . . ."**
   a. Walk between the taped lines on the floor (taped lines gradually get narrower, from 12 to 4 inches.
   b. Walk down an 8-inch-wide board.
   c. Walk down a 6-inch-wide board.
   d. Walk down a 4-inch-wide board.
   e. Walk down the board and step over the beanbag (or eraser) on the board.
   f. Walk down the board with your hands on your head.
   g. Variation: Walk on board to music.

4. **introduce self-initiated learning activities.** Set up the equipment (mats, boards, beams) and space for dynamic balancing. Provide time at the beginning of the lesson and free time for independent learning after the child understands the skills to be used. You may ask the child to create a game activity to play alone or with others (partner or small group) on and around the equipment.

5. **Variations:** Set up an obstacle course that includes colored tape, obstacles. Play a game, such as Beanbag Relay, Ice Cream Cone Game, or Do What I Do, that incorporates dynamic-balancing activities.

Performance Objective

The child with acquisition of Skill Level 1 can walk on a 4-inch-wide balance beam elevated 4–6 inches three consecutive times, demonstrating the following skill components:

On a balance beam, the child can

3. stand on elevated beam and move forward 8 feet in any manner without falling off beam and then

4. alternate feet while walking at least six steps without falling off beam.

Skills to Review

1. Stand on balance beam on floor and move forward 8 feet in any manner without falling off board and then

2. alternate feet while walking forward at least six steps without falling off board.

Action Words

Action: Go, stand, step, stop, walk

Objects: Beanbag, board, foot, lines

Concepts: Backward, forward, look, off, on, ready, show me, up

Games

- Beanbag Relay
- Did You Ever See a Lassie/Laddie?
- Do What I Do
- Follow the Leader
- Ice Cream Cone Game
- Ladder Game
- Obstacle Course
- Simon Says

TEACHING ACTIVITIES

If a child requires assistance to respond,

1. give verbal cues and physical assistance.
Manipulate or guide the child through the entire skill. Stand behind the child on the board. Walk the child across the board by holding him or her around the waist for support and moving one foot forward and then the other foot. Give the child specific verbal instructions throughout (in sign language, bliss symbols, action cues), such as "Walk across the beam," "Don't look at your feet," "Go."

2. give verbal cues with demonstration.
Use a model or have the child watch you walk across the 4-inch-wide beam with your arms extended out at shoulder height and looking forward. Then have the child perform the action. Use specific verbal instructions (as in 1 above with the modeling).

If a child can respond without assistance,

3. give a verbal challenge in the form of a problem: "Who can . . . ?" "Show me how you can . . ."

a. Walk on the colored tape on the beam.

b. Walk along the beam, focusing on the clown picture on the wall in front of you.

c. Walk along the path of the balance beam and step over the beanbags.

d. Walk up and down the beam incline.

e. Carry an eraser (beanbag) as you walk on the beam. Place the object on your head while you walk.

f. Variations: Walk on beam to music. Walk on colored footprints showing alternating feet along the beam.

4. introduce self-initiated learning activities. Set up the equipment (mats, boards, beams) and space for dynamic balancing. Provide time at the beginning of the lesson and free time for independent learning after the child understands the skills to be used. You may ask the child to create a game activity to play alone or with others (partner or small group) on and around the equipment.

5. Variations: Set up an obstacle course that includes colored tape, obstacles. Play a game, such as Beanbag Relay, Ice Cream Cone Game, or Do What I Do, that incorporates dynamic-balancing activities.

DYNAMIC BALANCING: SKILL LEVEL 3

Performance Objective

The child with acquisition of Skill Level 2 or a level of performance appropriate for the child's level of functioning can maintain that level over six weeks.

Given activities that require the skill, the child can

1. play two or more games listed below at home or school, and
2. play with equipment selected by teacher and parent(s).

Skills to Review

1. Level 1 dynamic balancing. Stand on balance beam on floor and move forward 8 feet in any manner without falling off board and then
2. alternate feet while walking forward at least six steps without falling off board.
3. Level 2 dynamic balancing. Stand on elevated beam and move forward 8 feet in any manner without falling off beam and then
4. alternate feet while walking at least six steps without falling off beam.

Action Words

Actions: Go, stand, step, stop, walk

Objects: Beanbag, board, foot, lines

Concepts: Backward, forward, look, off, on, ready, show me, up

Games

- Beanbag Relay
- Did You Ever See a Lassie/Laddie?
- Do What I Do
- Follow the Leader
- Ice Cream Cone Game
- Ladder Game
- Obstacle Course
- Simon Says

TEACHING ACTIVITIES FOR MAINTENANCE

In Teaching

1. Provide the child with teaching cues (verbal and nonverbal, such as demonstration, modeling, imitating) for dynamic balancing that involve the skill components the child has achieved in compatible teaching and play activities. Bring to the child's attention the skill components he or she has already achieved. Provide positive reinforcement and feedback for the child.

2. Use games that require dynamic balancing and that involve imitating, modeling, and demonstrating.

3. Observe and assess each child's maintenance at the end of two weeks. Repeat at the end of four weeks (if maintained) and six weeks after initial date of attainment.

▲ Box in the skill level to be maintained on the child's Class Record of Progress. Note the date the child attained target level of performance (defined by teacher alone or co-planned with parents).

▲ Two weeks after attainment, observe the child. Is the level maintained? If child does not demonstrate the skill components at the desired level of performance, indicate the skill components that need reteaching or reinforcing in the comments sheet on the Class Record of Progress. Reschedule teaching time, and co-plan with parents the home activities necessary to reinforce child's achievement of the skill components and maintenance of attainment.

▲ Continue to observe the child, and reteach and reinforce until the child maintains that level of performance for six weeks.

▲ Plan teaching activities incorporating these components so that the child can continually use and reinforce them and can acquire new ones over the year.

▲ When the child can understand it, make a check-list poster illustrating the child's achievements. Bring the child's attention to these skill components in various compatible play and game activities throughout the year. Have the child help others—a partner or a small group.

In Co-Planning with Parent(s)

1. Encourage the parent(s) to reinforce the child's achievement of the skill components in everyday play and living activities in the home.

▲ Provide key action words for the parent(s) to emphasize.

▲ Give the parent(s) a list of play and games to use in playing with the child, thus reinforcing the skill components the child has achieved and needs support to maintain.

▲ Give the parent(s) a list of dynamic-balancing activities that can be done at home with the child, such as

   a. Walking on the benches around the sandbox.

   b. Walking up and down the teeter-totter.

   c. Walking along the log at the park.

   d. Walking on the curb on the street.

   e. Walking on cracks in the sidewalk.

   f. Walking on the wooden blocks around the trees in the path.

   g. Walking on the sandbox ledge.

   h. Walking on the beam with a beanbag and tossing it from hand to hand as you move.

   i. Bouncing a ball inside hoops lined up next to beam as you walk on beam.

   j. Walking to the center of a beam with another child (both coming from different ends of beam), passing each other, and continuing to end of beam.

2. Set up a time every two weeks to interact with the parent(s) and exchange feedback on the child's progress.

PARACHUTE: SKILL LEVEL 1

Performance Objective

The child can perform three basic parachute activities with group three consecutive times, demonstrating the following skill components:

Within a clear space of 30 feet, the child can

1. assume ready position, face chute, reach down, grasp chute's edge with both hands (palms down), raise chute to waist level, and

2. shake chute, making the chute move up and down (ripple), and then

3. kneel, then stand up and raise chute high by extending arms overhead, take four steps in and look up inside the mushroom, and then turn around to face away from center and pull parachute down over head like umbrella.

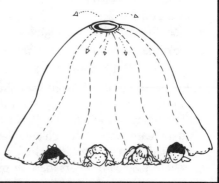

Action Words

Actions: Grasp, kneel, pull, raise, reach, ripple, stand, step, turn

Objects: Arm, balls, head, mushroom, parachute, umbrella

Concepts: Center, down, look, middle, ready, ready position, show me, up

Games

- Birds, Beasts, and Fish
- Capture the Bacon
- Car Races
- Cat and Rat
- Color Pick-up
- Find the Figure
- Gathering Objects
- Name Change
- Parachute Golf
- Popcorn
- Potpourri
- Rollerball
- Simon Says
- Snake Tag
- The Chase

TEACHING ACTIVITIES

If a child requires assistance to respond,

1. give verbal cues and physical assistance.
Manipulate or guide the child through the entire skill. (1) For beginning procedure, stand behind child and have him or her reach down, grasp chute's edge with both hands, using overhand grip, and bring parachute up to waist level. Give the child specific verbal instructions throughout (in sign language, bliss symbols, action cues), such as "Reach down, grasp chute, pull it to your waist," "Ready." (2) For umbrella and mushroom, stand behind the child and tell him or her to face parachute, squat on knees, grasp edge with two hands, using overhand grip. On "go," all stand up and raise parachute high by throwing arms straight up and overhead, then take four steps into middle and look up inside mushroom. Give the child specific verbal instructions throughout (in sign language, bliss symbols, action cues), such as "On knees, grasp chute, stand and raise chute up (umbrella), step in, mushroom." (3) For ripples and waves, stand behind child and have him or her reach

down, grasp edge with two hands, bring to waist, and shake or ripple the chute up and down. Give the child specific verbal instructions throughout (in sign language, bliss symbols, action cues), such as "Reach down, grasp chute, hold at your waist, shake hard."

2. give verbal cues with demonstration.
Use a model or have the child watch you demonstrate the beginning procedure, umbrella, mushroom, and ripples. Then have the child perform the action. Use specific verbal instructions (as in 1 above with the modeling).

If a child can respond without assistance,

3. give a verbal challenge in the form of a problem: "Who can . . . ?" "Show me how you can . . ."
a. Hold the parachute up high like an umbrella.
b. Hold the parachute up high like a mushroom.
c. Variation: Raise parachute to beat of music.

4. introduce self-initiated learning activities.
Set up the parachute and space for it. Provide time at the beginning of the lesson and free time for independent learning after the child understands the skills to be used. You may ask the child to create a game activity to play with others (partner or small group) on or around the equipment.

5. Variations: Set up parachute and play a game such as Snake Tag, Cat and Rat, or Name Change, that incorporates parachute activities.

PARACHUTE: SKILL LEVEL 2

Performance Objective

The child with acquisition of Skill Level 1 can perform locomotor and ball-handling skills with the parachute three consecutive times, demonstrating the following skill components:

Within a clear space of 30 feet, the child can

4. assume ready position, turn to right or left and, with other children, run, walk, or slide (locomotor skills), holding the chute, and

5. assume ready position with chute, throw ball (ball-handling skills) on or under the chute, and with other children, start rippling chute.

Skills to Review

1. Assume ready position, face chute, reach down, grasp chute's edge with both hands (palms down), raise chute to waist level, and

2. shake chute, making the chute move up and down (ripple), and then

3. kneel, then stand up and raise chute high by extending arms overhead, take four steps in and look up inside the mushroom, and then turn around and face away from center and pull parachute down over head like umbrella.

Action Words

Actions: Grasp, kneel, pull, raise, reach, ripple, stand, step, turn

Objects: Arm, balls, head, mushroom, parachute, umbrella

Concepts: Center, down, look, middle, ready, ready position, show me, up

Games

- Birds, Beasts, and Fish
- Capture the Bacon
- Car Races
- Cat and Rat
- Color Pick-up
- Find the Figure
- Gathering Objects
- Name Change
- Parachute Golf
- Popcorn
- Potpourri
- Rollerball
- Simon Says
- Snake Tag
- The Chase

TEACHING ACTIVITIES

If a child requires assistance to respond,

1. give verbal cues and physical assistance.
Manipulate or guide the child through the entire skill. *For gross motor skills,* assist child in bringing parachute up to waist level, ready position. Turn child to right or left and run (and other locomotor skills) alongside as child continues to hold parachute. Give the child specific verbal instructions throughout (in sign language, bliss symbols, action cues), such as "Reach down, grasp chute, pull it to your waist," "Run with it," "Hold it tight." *For ball skills,* manipulate and guide the child through the skill. (1) Stand behind the child and have him or her grasp the chute's edge with both hands, using overhand grip, and bring parachute to waist level. Shake hard. (2) Throw ball on top of chute and assist child in shaking or rippling the chute up and down, keeping ball on chute. Give the child specific verbal instructions throughout (in sign language, bliss symbols, action cues), such as "Watch the ball move," "Raise the chute up and down," "Shake hard," "Keep the ball on the chute."

2. give verbal cues with demonstration.
Use a model or have the child watch you demonstrate the ready position and running (or other locomotor skill) with parachute in one hand. Demonstrate ready position. Then have the child perform the action. Use specific verbal instructions (as in 1 above with the modeling).

If a child can respond without assistance,

3. give a verbal challenge in the form of a problem: "Who can . . . ?" "Show me how you can . . ."

a. Hold the parachute in ready position and run (jump, hop, skip, slide, etc.) with the chute in one hand.

b. Hold the parachute in ready position and ripple it so that the ball bounces like popcorn.

c. Hold the parachute in ready position and throw a ball under chute. Try to catch someone else's ball.

d. Hold the parachute in ready position and roll the ball around the edge of the parachute.

e. Variations: Roll balls on parachute to music. Run, skip, jump with parachute in hand to music.

4. introduce self-initiated learning activities.
Set up the parachute and space for it. Provide time at the beginning of the lesson and free time for independent learning after the child understands the skills to be used. You may ask the child to create a game activity to play with others (partner or small group) on or around the equipment.

5. Variations: Set up parachute and play a game, such as Snake Tag, Cat and Rat, or Name Change, that incorporates parachute activities.

PARACHUTE: SKILL LEVEL 3

Performance Objective

The child with acquisition of Skill Level 2 or a level of performance appropriate for the child's level of functioning can maintain that level over six weeks.

Given activities that require the skill, the child can

1. play two or more games listed below at home or school, and
2. play with equipment selected by teacher and parent(s).

Skills to Review

1. Level 1 parachute. Assume ready position, face chute, reach down, grasp chute's edge with both hands (palms down), raise chute to waist level, and
2. shake chute, making the chute move up and down (ripple), and then
3. kneel, then stand up and raise chute high by extending arms overhead, take four steps in and look up inside the mushroom, and then turn around and face away from center and pull parachute down over head like umbrella.
4. Level 2 parachute. Assume ready position, turn to right or left and, with other children, run, walk, or slide (locomotor skills), holding the chute and then
5. assume ready position with chute, throw ball (ball-handling skills) on or under the chute and, with other children, start rippling the chute.

Action Words

Actions: Grasp, kneel, pull, raise, reach, ripple, stand, step, turn

Objects: Arm, balls, head, mushroom, parachute, umbrella

Concepts: Center, down, look, middle, ready, ready position, show me, up

Games

- Birds, Beasts, and Fish
- Capture the Bacon
- Car Races
- Cat and Rat
- Color Pick-up
- Find the Figure
- Gathering Objects
- Name Change
- Parachute Golf
- Popcorn
- Potpourri
- Rollerball
- Simon Says
- Snake Tag
- The Chase

TEACHING ACTIVITIES FOR MAINTENANCE

In Teaching

1. Provide the child with teaching cues (verbal and nonverbal, such as demonstration, modeling, imitating) for parachute play that involve the skill components the child has achieved in compatible teaching and play activities. Bring to the child's attention the skill components he or she has already achieved. Provide positive reinforcement and feedback for the child.

2. Use games that require parachute playing and that involve imitating, modeling, and demonstrating.

3. Observe and assess each child's maintenance at the end of two weeks. Repeat at the end of four weeks (if maintained) and six weeks after initial date of attainment.

▲ Box in the skill level to be maintained on the child's Class Record of Progress. Note the date the child attained target level of performance (defined by teacher alone or co-planned with parents).

▲ Two weeks after attainment, observe the child. Is the level maintained? If child does not demonstrate the skill components at the desired level of performance, indicate the skill components that need reteaching or reinforcing in the comments sheet on the Class Record of Progress. Reschedule teaching time, and co-plan with parents the home activities necessary to reinforce child's achievement of the skill components and maintenance of attainment.

▲ Continue to observe the child, and reteach and reinforce until the child maintains that level of performance for six weeks.

▲ Plan teaching activities incorporating these components so that the child can continually use and reinforce them and can acquire new ones over the year.

▲ When the child can understand it, make a checklist poster illustrating the child's achievements. Bring the child's attention to these skill components in various compatible play and game activities throughout the year. Have the child help others—a partner or a small group.

In Co-Planning with Parent(s)

1. Encourage the parent(s) to reinforce the child's achievement of the skill components in everyday play and living activities in the home.

▲ Provide key action words for the parent(s) to emphasize.

▲ Give the parent(s) a list of play and games to use in playing with the child, thus reinforcing the skill components the child has achieved and needs support to maintain. Demonstrate use of sheet or blanket as a substitute parachute.

2. Set up a time every two weeks to interact with the parent(s) and exchange feedback on the child's progress.

Checklists:
Individual and Class Records of Progress

A checklist is an objective score sheet for each stunt and tumbling skill taught in the program. By observing and assessing each child's level of performance, you can identify the activities that will assist the child in reaching the performance objective. Use the same checklist to monitor the child's progress during instruction. When the child's performance level changes, you can upgrade the learning tasks (skill components) to the child's new skill level.

To Begin

Decide on one or more stunt and tumbling activities to be taught in the program. Become familiar with the description of the performance objective for each activity selected. Review the scoring key on the checklist. Plan assessing activities for the selected skills. The number will depend on the class size, the needs of the children, and the help available to you. Set up testing stations similar to the learning stations. Some teachers use free-play time (after setting up equipment for the objective to be tested) to observe the children.

1. Begin assessing at Skill Level 2 for the particular objective. If the child cannot perform at Skill Level 2, assess for Skill Level 1. If the child demonstrates the skill components for Skill Level 2 (i.e., with modeling, verbal cues, or no cues), the child has achieved functional competence. At the next skill level, Skill Level 3, the child demonstrates maintenance retention of the skill over time.

2. For some children with special needs, you may need to assess their levels of functioning before planning teaching activities. As in step 1, observe and assess the amount and type of assistance (cues) the child needs in descending order (i.e., from verbal cues to total manipulation).

Code	Amount and Type of Assistance
SI	Child initiates demonstrating the skill in the teaching and playing of activities
C	Child demonstrates the skill when given verbal cues with or without demonstration
A	Child demonstrates the skill when given partial assistance or total manipulation throughout the execution of the skill

Record, using the code above, the child's initial assistance level and progress in the comments column of the Class Record of Progress. For some children, this may be the most significant initial progress noted (i.e., from assistance to verbal cues and demonstration).

To Assess

1. Be sure all children are working on objectives at other stations while you are assessing at one station.

2. Make sure enough equipment is available for the skill to be tested.

3. For log roll, forward roll, and backward roll, have 3 or 4 children line up at end of mat. All other children should be working at other learning stations. Have each child take a turn on the command "go." At the end of the trials, record the child's performance on the score sheet.

4. For static balance, have 3 or 4 children, one at a time, stand on the balance board or on a line on the ground. Each child takes a turn on the command "go." At the end of the trials, record the child's performance on the score sheet.

5. For dynamic balancing, have 3 or 4 children line up at the end of the beam. One by one, each child takes a turn walking across the beam. On the command "go," have children perform the skills. At the end of the trials, record the child's performance on the score sheet.

6. For parachute activities, have children line up around the parachute. On the command "go," have the children perform skills. The teacher must match the children individually and record each child's progress on the score sheet.

7. You may need to modify the assessing activity for children's special needs by using spotters, taking a child through the pattern or modeling the activity, or using sign language or an interpreter. Other modifications are an individual structured assessment with no distractions from other children or activities or free play with the equipment. Use mats or movable walls to help cut down on distractions.

To Adapt the Checklists

You can note children's skill components adaptations (i.e., physical devices or other changes) in the comments column on the Class Record of Progress. Other changes can be written under recommendations for individual children or the class. Modifications made for a child can be noted on the Individual Record of Progress. The Class Record of Progress can be adapted for an individual child. Record the name of the child rather than the class, and in the name column, record assessment dates. This adaptation may be needed for children whose progress is erratic, because it provides a base line assessment to find out where to begin teaching and evaluating the child's progress.

The Individual Record of Progress for the end-of-the-year report can be attached to the child's IEP (Individual Education Program)

report. The record can also serve as a cumulative record for each child. Such records are very useful for new teachers, substitute teachers, aides, and volunteers, as well as parents. The format of the Individual Record of Progress can also be adapted for a Unit Report. The names of all the objectives for a unit— for example, walk-run endurance, running, catching a ball, and rolling a ball—are written rather than the names of the children. Book 8 illustrates the adaptation of the Individual Record of Progress for use in the Home Activities Program and for a Unit Report.

The checklists may be reproduced as needed to implement the play and motor skills program.

Class Record of Progress Report

Class _____   Date _____

Age/grade _____   Teacher _____

School _____

Objective: Log Roll

SCORING:	SKILL LEVEL 1		SKILL LEVEL 2		SKILL LEVEL 3	PRIMARY RESPONSES:
ASSESSMENT: _____Date **X** = Achieved **O** = Not Achieved / = Partially Achieved REASSESSMENT: _____Date ⊗ = Achieved ∅ = Not Achieved	Three Consecutive Times					N = Not Attending NR = No Response UR = Unrelated Response O = Other (Specify in comments)
	Rolls from front to back, keeping arms extended overhead and legs together.	Rolls from back to front, keeping arms extended overhead and legs together.	Rolls from front to back to front, with arms extended overhead and legs together.	Rolls from back to front to back, with arms extended overhead and legs together.	Two or more play or game activities at home or school demonstrating skill components over six-week period.	
NAME	1	2	3	4	5	COMMENTS
1.						
2.						
3.						
4.						
5.						
6.						
7.						
8.						
9.						
10.						

Recommendations: Specific changes or conditions in planning for instructions, performance, or diagnostic testing procedures or standards. Please describe what worked best.

_____

_____

_____

_____

_____

Class Record of Progress Report

CLASS _____ DATE _____

AGE/GRADE _____ TEACHER _____

SCHOOL _____

OBJECTIVE: FORWARD ROLL

SCORING:	SKILL LEVEL 1			SKILL LEVEL 2	SKILL LEVEL 3	PRIMARY RESPONSES:
ASSESSMENT: _____ Date **X** = Achieved **O** = Not Achieved **/** = Partially Achieved REASSESSMENT: _____ Date **⊗** = Achieved **Ø** = Not Achieved	Three Consecutive Times					N = Not Attending NR = No Response UR = Unrelated Response O = Other (Specify in comments)
	Kneels or squats with hands on mat near head, palms down.	Tucks chin down near chest, rounds back, holding knees slightly apart and close to chin.	Rolls forward across back to sitting position in two or more rolls.	Pushes with hands, palms down on mat, and rolls forward in tight tuck position to sitting or standing position.	Two or more play or game activities at home or school demonstrating skill components over six-week period.	
NAME	1	2	3	4	5	COMMENTS
1.						
2.						
3.						
4.						
5.						
6.						
7.						
8.						
9.						
10.						

Recommendations: Specific changes or conditions in planning for instructions, performance, or diagnostic testing procedures or standards. Please describe what worked best.

_____

_____

_____

_____

_____

CLASS RECORD OF PROGRESS REPORT

CLASS _____ DATE _____

AGE/GRADE _____ TEACHER _____

SCHOOL _____

OBJECTIVE: BACKWARD ROLL

NAME	SKILL LEVEL 1 — Three Consecutive Times			SKILL LEVEL 2		SKILL LEVEL 3	COMMENTS
	Sits down, close to heels, knees slightly apart and close to chin, hands with palms up, and rolls backward.	Keeping body in tight tuck position (chin tucked, back rounded, knees close to chin) rolls across mat, palms on mat, thumbs near head.	Comes to sitting position with feet on mat, arms at sides, chin tucked in.	With palms on mat, thumbs toward head, pushes against mat to complete the roll (backward momentum), body in tight tuck.	Lands on feet and stands, maintaining balance, or makes two or more continuous rolls.	Two or more play or game activities at home or school demonstrating skill components over six-week period.	
	1	2	3	4	5	6	
1.							
2.							
3.							
4.							
5.							
6.							
7.							
8.							
9.							
10.							

Recommendations: Specific changes or conditions in planning for instructions, performance, or diagnostic testing procedures or standards. Please describe what worked best.

_____

_____

_____

_____

_____

CLASS RECORD OF PROGRESS REPORT

CLASS _____ DATE _____

AGE/GRADE _____ TEACHER _____

SCHOOL _____

OBJECTIVE: STATIC BALANCING

SCORING:	SKILL LEVEL 1			SKILL LEVEL 2			SKILL LEVEL 3	PRIMARY RESPONSES:
ASSESSMENT:	Three Consecutive Times							N = Not Attending
_____Date								NR = No Response
X = Achieved	Stands on 4-inch line in forward stride position, with arms extended out, head up and facing forward.	Stands on 6-inch-wide board on floor in forward stride position, with arms extended and parallel to floor, head up and facing forward.	Stands on 4-inch-wide board on floor in forward stride position, with arms extended and parallel to floor, head up and facing forward.	Stands on floor with both feet together, then bends one leg so that leg is up and back, arms extended, head up and looking forward.	Stands on floor with both feet together, then bends one leg so that foot can be placed inside knee of support leg, arms extended, head up and looking forward.	Stands on a 4-inch-wide board or line in forward stride position, bends rear leg up and back, with arms extended, head up and looking forward.	Two or more play or game activities at home or school demonstrating skill components over six-week period.	UR = Unrelated Response
O = Not Achieved								O = Other (Specify in comments)
/ = Partially Achieved								
REASSESSMENT:								
_____Date								
⊗ = Achieved								
Ø = Not Achieved								

NAME	1	2	3	4	5	6	7	COMMENTS
1.								
2.								
3.								
4.								
5.								
6.								
7.								
8.								
9.								
10.								

Recommendations: Specific changes or conditions in planning for instructions, performance, or diagnostic testing procedures or standards. Please describe what worked best.

_____

_____

_____

_____

_____

Class Record of Progress Report

CLASS _____   DATE _____

AGE/GRADE _____   TEACHER _____

SCHOOL _____

OBJECTIVE: DYNAMIC BALANCING

SCORING:	SKILL LEVEL 1		SKILL LEVEL 2		SKILL LEVEL 3	PRIMARY RESPONSES:
ASSESSMENT: _____Date **X** = Achieved **O** = Not Achieved **/** = Partially Achieved REASSESSMENT: _____Date ⊗ = Achieved Ø = Not Achieved	Three Consecutive Times					N = Not Attending NR = No Response UR = Unrelated Response O = Other (Specify in comments)
	Stands on balance beam on floor and moves forward 8 feet in any manner without falling off board.	Alternates feet while walking forward at least six steps without falling off board.	Stands on elevated beam and moves forward 8 feet in any manner without falling off board.	Alternates feet while walking at least six steps without falling off beam.	Two or more play or game activities at home or school demonstrating skill components over six-week period.	
NAME	1	2	3	4	5	COMMENTS
1.						
2.						
3.						
4.						
5.						
6.						
7.						
8.						
9.						
10.						

Recommendations: Specific changes or conditions in planning for instructions, performance, or diagnostic testing procedures or standards. Please describe what worked best.

_____

_____

_____

_____

_____

CLASS RECORD OF PROGRESS REPORT

CLASS _____ DATE _____

AGE/GRADE _____ TEACHER _____

SCHOOL _____

OBJECTIVE: PARACHUTE

SCORING:	SKILL LEVEL 1			SKILL LEVEL 2		SKILL LEVEL 3	PRIMARY RESPONSES:
ASSESSMENT: _____Date **X** = Achieved **O** = Not Achieved / = Partially Achieved REASSESSMENT: _____Date ⊗ = Achieved Ø = Not Achieved	Three Consecutive Times						N = Not Attending NR = No Response UR = Unrelated Response O = Other (Specify in comments)
	Assumes ready position, faces chute, reaches down, grasps chute's edge with both hands (palms down), raises chute to waist level.	Shakes chute, making the chute move up and down (ripple).	Raises chute high overhead, like a mushroom, and then pulls chute down over head like umbrella.	In ready position, turns to right or left and, with other children, runs, walks, or slides (locomotor skills), holding the chute.	Assumes ready position with chute, throws ball (ball-handling skills) on or under chute and, with other children, starts rippling chute.	Two or more play or game activities at home or school demonstrating skill components over six-week period.	
NAME	1	2	3	4	5	6	COMMENTS
1.							
2.							
3.							
4.							
5.							
6.							
7.							
8.							
9.							
10.							

Recommendations: Specific changes or conditions in planning for instructions, performance, or diagnostic testing procedures or standards. Please describe what worked best.

_____

_____

_____

_____

_____

INDIVIDUAL RECORD OF PROGRESS

Area: Stunts and Tumbling

CHILD: _____

LEVEL: _____

YEAR: _____

TEACHER: _____

SCHOOL: _____

Marking Period	Date
Fall Conference (white)	from____to____
Winter Conference (yellow)	from____to____
Spring Conference (pink)	from____to____
End-of-Year (cumulative) Report (blue)	from____to____

Preprimary Play and Motor Skills Activity Program

The Individual Record of Progress lists all of the objectives in which your child receives instruction during the play and motor skills program. The information reported on your child's Individual Record of Progress shows your child's entry performance and progress for a marking period. The end-of-the-year report represents your child's Individual Education Program (IEP) for the objectives selected and taught during the year.

Each objective is broken into small, measurable steps or skill components. This assists the teacher to assess what your child already knew before teaching began and to determine which step to start teaching first. One of the following symbols is marked by each step or skill component of the objective:

X = The child already knew how to perform this step before teaching it began.

O = The child did not know how to perform this step before teaching it began or after instruction of it ended.

⊘ = The child did not know how to perform this step before teaching it began, but did learn how to do it during the instruction period.

This information should be helpful to you in planning home activities to strengthen your child's play and motor skills.

Comments

_____

_____

_____

_____

_____

_____

_____

_____

LOG ROLL

Date: _____

On an 8-foot mat
Three consecutive times

—— Rolls from front to back, keeping arms extended overhead and legs together.

—— Rolls from back to front, keeping arms extended overhead and legs together.

—— Rolls from front to back to front, with arms extended overhead and legs together.

—— Rolls from back to front to back, with arms extended overhead and legs together.

—— Demonstrates above skill in two or more play or game activities at home or school over a six-week period.

FORWARD ROLL

Date: _____

On an 8-foot mat
Three consecutive times

—— Kneels or squats with hands on mat near head, palms down.

—— Tucks chin down near chest, rounds back, holding knees slightly apart and close to chin.

—— Rolls forward across back to sitting position in two or more rolls.

—— Pushes with hands, palms down on mat, and rolls forward in tight tuck position to sitting or standing position.

—— Demonstrates above skill in two or more play or game activities at home or school over a six-week period.

BACKWARD ROLL

Date: _____

On an 8-foot mat
Three consecutive times

_____ Sits down, close to heels, knees slightly apart and close to chin, hands with palms up, and rolls backward.

_____ Keeping body in tight tuck position (chin tucked, back rounded, knees close to chin), rolls across mat, palms on mat, thumbs near head.

_____ Comes to sitting position with feet on mat, arms at sides, chin tucked in.

_____ With palms on mat, thumbs toward head, pushes against mat to complete the roll (backward momentum), body in tight tuck.

_____ Lands on feet and stands, maintaining balance, or makes two or more continuous rolls.

_____ Demonstrates above skill in two or more play or game activities at home or school over a six-week period.

STATIC BALANCING

Date: _____

Within a clear space of 5 feet
Three consecutive times for 5 seconds

_____ Stands on 4-inch line in forward stride position (toes of rear foot touching heel of front foot), with arms extended out from shoulders and parallel to floor, head up and facing forward.

_____ Stands on a 6-inch board on floor in forward stride position (toes of rear foot touching heel of front foot), with arms extended out from shoulders and parallel to floor, head up and facing forward.

_____ Stands on 4-inch-wide board on floor in forward stride position (toes of rear foot touching heel of front foot), with arms extended out from shoulders and parallel to floor, head up and facing forward.

_____ Stands on the floor with both feet together, then bends one leg so that lower leg is up and back (bent at a right angle), arms extended out from shoulders and parallel to floor and head up and looking forward.

_____ Stands on the floor with both feet together, then bends one leg so that the foot can be placed inside knee of support leg, with arms extended out from shoulders and parallel to floor and head up and looking forward.

_____ Stands on a 4-inch-wide board or line in forward stride position, bends rear leg so that lower leg is up and back, arms extended out from shoulders, head up and looking forward.

_____ Demonstrates above skill in two or more play or game activities at home or school over a six-week period.

DYNAMIC BALANCING

Date: _____

Within a clear space of 5 feet
Three consecutive times

____ Stands on balance beam on floor and moves forward 8 feet in any manner without falling off board.

____ Alternates feet while walking forward at least six steps without falling off board.

____ Stands on elevated beam and moves forward 8 feet in any manner without falling off board.

____ Alternates feet while walking at least six steps without falling off beam.

____ Demonstrates above skill in two or more play or game activities at home or school over a six-week period.

PARACHUTE

Date: _____

Within a space of 30 feet
Three basic parachute activities
Three consecutive times

____ Assumes ready position, faces chute, reaches down, grasps chute's edge with both hands (palms down), raises chute to waist level.

____ Shakes chute, making the chute move up and down (ripple).

____ Kneels, then stands up and raises chute high by extending arms overhead, takes four steps in and looks up inside the mushroom and then turns around and faces away from center and pulls chute down over head like umbrella.

____ Assumes ready position, turns to right or left and, with other children, runs, walks, or slides (locomotor skills), holding the chute.

____ Assumes ready position with chute, throws ball (ball-handling skills) on or under chute and, with other children, starts rippling chute.

____ Demonstrates above skill in two or more play or game activities at home or school over a six-week period.

Games

Game Selection

The following game sheets will help you select and plan game activities. They include the names of the games in alphabetical order, formation, directions, equipment, locomotor skills, and type of play activity. Consider the following points when selecting games:

1. Skills and objectives of your program

2. Interest of the child

3. Equipment and rules

4. Adaptability of physical difficulty level in order to match each child's ability

5. Activity for healthy growth and development

6. Social play skill development, such as taking turns, sharing equipment, playing with others, and following and leading

Games can foster creativity. Children enjoy making up, interpreting, and creating their own activities, whether playing alone, with a partner, or with a small group. The time you take to provide opportunities for each child to explore and create will be well spent. One further note. Children can easily create or adapt games matched to their mobility, even if limited by crutches, braces, or wheelchairs. Stunts and tumbling activities involve moving from here to there. These children easily comprehend how to get to "there" with their own expertise for movement.

Following are some suggestions for adapting the physical difficulty level of games and a sequential list of social play development.

Adapting Games

To Change	Use	Example
1. Boundaries	Larger or smaller space	In Rolling Races, increase distance of the roll.
2. Equipment	Larger or smaller sizes, weights, or heights, or specially adapted equipment for some children (such as guide-rails, inclines rather than stairs, brightly colored mats)	Use variously graduated inclines (can make with mats).
3. Rules	More or fewer rules	In Run and Roll, start with one roll, then increase number of rolls on mat.

To Change	Use	Example
4. Actions	More or fewer actions to be performed at one time; play in stationary positions, using various body parts	Balance on one or more body part at a time, playing the game Do What I Do.
5. Time of play	Longer or shorter time; frequent rest periods	In Balancing Fun, increase time of the balance.

To adapt games to other special needs, you might also use buddies and spotters, sign language gestures, or place the child near leader.

Sequential Development of Social Play

Sequence	Description	Example of Play Activity
Individual Play	Child plays alone and independently with toys that are different from those used by other children within speaking distance.	Child rolls on mat or rug. Other children roll on other rugs or mats.
Parallel Play	Child plays independently beside, rather than with, other children.	Child performs static balance stunts in the room; other children are doing the same thing—no interaction.
Associate Play	Child plays with other children. There is interaction between children, but there are no common goals.	Children perform balancing stunts at the same time and follow one another.
Cooperative Play	Child plays within a group organized for playing formal games. Group is goal directed.	Children play Parachute Golf and Snake Tag together, cooperatively sharing the same goals.

GAME SHEET LESSON PLANS

GAMES	ORGANIZATION	DESCRIPTION/INSTRUCTIONS	EQUIPMENT	SKILLS	TYPE OF PLAY ACTIVITY
Balancing Fun	Scattered X X X X X X X X	Each child finds a spot on mat. Say, "We're going to balance. Try not to fall over. Who can balance on one leg and one arm? What other two points can you balance on?" Have children show their different balances.	Mats	Balances: 2 points and 1 point	Individual, partners, small group, large group
Birds, Beasts, and Fish	All around parachute (circle with X's around it)	Count off children by threes: birds are 1, beasts are 2, fish are 3. Raise chute and call out birds, beasts, or fish. All those with that number must run under chute and change places before chute comes down.	Parachute	Parachute	Small group, large group
Beanbag Relay	Lines x x x x →□ x x x x →□	Divide children into teams. Encourage them to carry beanbags on body parts (head, shoulders, hands, etc.) as they move to put beanbags into container. First team back wins.	Beanbags; baskets or boxes	Dynamic balancing	Relay; small group, large group

GAME SHEET LESSON PLANS

GAMES	ORGANIZATION	DESCRIPTION/INSTRUCTIONS	EQUIPMENT	SKILLS	TYPE OF PLAY ACTIVITY
Capture the Bacon	All around parachute	Have equal number of children assigned number. Put beanbag under chute. When number is called, try to capture the bacon (beanbag) and return to spot before chute descends. Points are awarded to ones capturing the bacon.	Parachute; beanbag	Parachute	Teams; small group, large group
Car Races	All around parachute	Choose group leader. Children count off in groups of three. All with same number are same kind of car. Leader calls out name of car and all those "cars" run around outside of parachute to original spot (garage) and then tap leader in center.	Parachute	Parachute	Teams; small group, large group
Cat and Rat	All around parachute	All bring chute up. One cat and one rat are selected. Cat is outside chute circle and rat is inside. The cat says, "I'm the cat." The rat says, "I'm the rat." The cat, "I will catch you." The rat, "No, you can't." The cat then chases rat to trap it. All holding chute try to protect rat. Rat can come and go as it wishes. Others try to keep cat outside by using their bodies to block it. When cat taps rat, cat becomes rat and another child becomes cat.	Parachute	Parachute	Small group, large group

Game Sheet Lesson Plans

Games	Organization	Description/Instructions	Equipment	Skills	Type of Play Activity
Color Pick-up	All around parachute	Assign a different color to each child, and place several beanbags in center under chute. When parachute is inflated into umbrella, call a color. All children with that color retrieve at least one beanbag before chute touches them.	Parachute; beanbags	Parachute	Small group, large group
Did You Ever See a Lassie/Laddie?	Line / semicircle	Leader starts song, performs activity. Children mimic movement.	Bar, beam, ladder, mats, stairs, boxes, handrails, incline ramp	Log roll, forward roll, static balance, dynamic balance	Small group, large group
Do What I Do	Scattered	Teacher says, "Watch me. Do what I do." Use simple actions that children can perform, including rolls and balances, as many times as you wish. Say, "This is what I can do. I think you can do it too. This is what I can do. Now I pass it on to you."	Mats	All rolls, all balances	Individual, partners, small group, large group

GAME SHEET LESSON PLANS

GAMES	ORGANIZATION	DESCRIPTION/INSTRUCTIONS	EQUIPMENT	SKILLS	TYPE OF PLAY ACTIVITY
Find the Figure	All around parachute	Inflate parachute over variety of shapes. When leader shows shape, select one or two children to run under chute to match shape before chute descends.	Parachute; variety of geometric shapes	Parachute	Small group, large group
Follow the Drum Beat	Lines	Each child stands on a line 6 feet long. Say, "Take a step each time I beat the drum. Walk forward—(beat, beat, beat)—turn—walk back to start." Change tempo to fast or slow.	Drum; tape	Dynamic balance	Individual, partners, small group, large group
Follow the Leader	Line, circle	Leader performs action. Children respond by mimicking action.	Mats, rugs, parachutes, cones	All stunts and tumbling skills	Partners, small group

Game Sheet Lesson Plans

Games	Organization	Description/Instructions	Equipment	Skills	Type of Play Activity
Freeze Balance Tag	Scattered	Have children balance themselves on mat, using one body part in contact with mat, then two body parts (arm and leg), then three body parts. Hold position for count of 5. Can also try on playground apparatuses.	Mats	Static balancing	Small group
Gathering Objects	All around parachute	All children in ready position. Choose a leader, and give each child a different number or color. Place objects under chute. Call two names, colors, or numbers. Two children go under to see how many objects they can find and carry out before chute touches them.	Parachute; bean-bags; deflated balls	Parachute	Small group, large group
Hopscotch	Line	Encourage children to draw hopscotch board on sidewalk. Demonstrate hopping on one foot in single square, two feet in double square.	Chalk, tape	Static balancing	Small group

GAME SHEET LESSON PLANS

GAMES	ORGANIZATION	DESCRIPTION/INSTRUCTIONS	EQUIPMENT	SKILLS	TYPE OF PLAY ACTIVITY
Ice Cream Cone Game	Line	Have children stand on line next to each other with pretend ice cream cones. Walk to other side on board without dropping cone; walk back to start.	Balloons; paper cups; balance beams or boards	Dynamic balancing	Relay; small group, large group
Ladder Game	Line	Place ladder flat on floor. Children line up behind ladder. Have each child walk between rungs without stepping on them. Can have two ladders and a relay. Can walk on rungs or on sides of ladder.	Ladders	Dynamic balance	Individual, partners, small group, large group
Name Change	All around parachute	Number children in pairs. One child is "it" outside of chute. Bring chute up. On command, a number is called and the two with that number must change places before they are tagged by "it." A child who is tagged becomes "it."	Parachute	Parachute	Small group, large group

GAME SHEET LESSON PLANS

GAMES	ORGANIZATION	DESCRIPTION/INSTRUCTIONS	EQUIPMENT	SKILLS	TYPE OF PLAY ACTIVITY
Obstacle Course	Line + + + + T + + + + T semicircle + × + + × × × + + + × + × × ×	First child begins course; when first child completes second station, second student starts.	Parachutes, cones, mats, rugs, beams	All stunts and tumbling skills	Individual, partners, small group, large group
Parachute Golf	All around parachute	All in ready position. Put three plastic balls on chute. Try to shake chute so that balls pass through center hole. Can do this with two teams and two sets of different balls.	Parachute; balls	Parachute	Teams; small group, large group
Popcorn	All around parachute	All children hold chute at ready position. Try to keep balls thrown on top of chute popping by waving chute.	Parachute; balls	Parachute	Large group, small group

GAME SHEET LESSON PLANS

GAMES	ORGANIZATION	DESCRIPTION/INSTRUCTIONS	EQUIPMENT	SKILLS	TYPE OF PLAY ACTIVITY
Potpourri	All around parachute	Divide children into two teams, and number them off. When number is called, ask them to perform a task: bounce ball five times, crawl to opposite side, roll over three times, hop around inside of circle.	Parachute	Parachute	Teams; small group, large group
Roll and Toss	Scatter	Roll down a hill or incline with foam ball in hand. Throw ball into barrel, and run up incline (hill). Children also can run up incline to start.	Foam balls; barrel; hilly outdoor area	Roll	Small group, large group
Roll Away	Lines	First child in each line begins rolling down the mat on signal of "go." All roll in turn and then return to place in line.	Mats	All rolls, all balances	Individual, partners, small group, large group

Game Sheet Lesson Plans

GAMES	ORGANIZATION	DESCRIPTION/INSTRUCTIONS	EQUIPMENT	SKILLS	TYPE OF PLAY ACTIVITY
Rollerball	All around parachute	All children in ready position. Place ball on chute. All attempt to roll it around the outer edge of chute. Each child lowers chute as ball comes near and raises it as ball passes.	Parachute	Parachute	Small group, large group
Roll Like a Ball	Scatter	Children make themselves "into a ball," tucking their chin, arms, and legs tightly. Have them roll on mats or down grassy hills.	Grassy slope or tumbling mats	Roll	Individual, partners, small group, large group
Rolling Down Grassy Hills	Scatter	Children roll down grassy hills. See who gets to bottom first.	Grassy slope	Roll	Relays; individual, partners, small group, large group

GAME SHEET LESSON PLANS

GAMES	ORGANIZATION	DESCRIPTION/INSTRUCTIONS	EQUIPMENT	SKILLS	TYPE OF PLAY ACTIVITY
Rolling in Snow to Make Body Prints (Angels in Snow)	Scatter X X X X X X X X	Children (dressed warmly) lie down in the snow and roll to make prints, or swing arms to make "angel wings."	Snow	Roll	Individual, partners, small group, large group
Rolling Into/Out of a Blanket	Scatter X X X X X X X	Roll children in a blanket. Roll children out of blanket. Encourage children to roll themselves in and out. Relate activities to caterpillar, which goes into a cocoon and comes out a butterfly, by talking and movements.	Blankets or towels, tumbling mats	All rolls	Individual, partner, small group, large group

Game Sheet Lesson Plans

Games	Organization	Description/Instructions	Equipment	Skills	Type of Play Activity
Rolling Races	Lines x x x x x x	At signal, children begin rolling down incline. They stand up, run up incline, and sit at starting area.	Rug squares, inclined mat	All rolls	Relays; partners, small group, large group
Run and Roll	Circle forward — roll mat cone — cone mat forward	Divide children into two groups. Have them first walk through the procedure. Then they run around the cones and perform a forward roll on mats. Continue until whistle is blown.	2 traffic cones; mats (1 per 3 or 4 children)	Roll	Individual, partners, small group, large group

Game Sheet Lesson Plans

Games	Organization	Description/Instructions	Equipment	Skills	Type of Play Activity
Simon Says (with parachute)	All around parachute	Children raise chute to waist. Leader tells children, "Simon says drop chute below (or over) arm." If leader doesn't say "Simon," don't do action.	Parachute	Parachute	Small group, large group
Simon Says (balancing skills)	Semicircle	Demonstrate various body movements for children to imitate on "Simon says." Imitate actions only when they hear "Simon says."	None or selected for a specific skill	Static, dynamic balances	Partners, small group, large group

Game Sheet Lesson Plans

Games	Organization	Description/Instructions	Equipment	Skills	Type of Play Activity
Snake Tag	All around parachute	Place four long jump ropes on chute. Divide children into two teams. Have children make ripples and try to make snakes (ropes) touch children on other team.	Parachute; 4 long ropes	Parachute	Teams; small group, large group
Static Balance	Scatter	Spread students around room. Say, "Balance on two legs. Now hold hands over your head and balance to count of 5. Now balance on two legs and hold arms out like this."	None	2-point balance	Small group, large group

Game Sheet Lesson Plans

Games	Organization	Description/Instructions	Equipment	Skills	Type of Play Activity
Statue in the Garden	Scatter	Teacher says, "We are going to be statues in the garden. We must stand very still like this. Let's be statues. When music stops, we become statues."	Record player	2-point balance, 1-point balance	Individual, partners, small group, large group
Statues Moving	Scatter	Scatter children around room. Say, "Balance on two body points, one body part. Balance on one leg while I count to 5. Now hold your arms out. Balance to count of 5. Try your other leg."	None	1-point static balance	Individual, partners, small group, large group

Game Sheet Lesson Plans

Games	Organization	Description/Instructions	Equipment	Skills	Type of Play Activity
The Chase	All around parachute	One child is "it." The others raise chute. "It" walks around circle, holding sponge ball; puts ball behind first person. That person picks up ball and chases "it" around circle, trying to hit "it" with ball before "it" gets back to spot.	Parachute; sponge ball	Parachute	Small group, large group
Twister	Circle	Have children individually balance a part of their bodies on specific colors or shapes (e.g., 1 foot on circle, other on square). Have children close eyes when balancing.	Commercial twister game or different colored cutouts placed on floor	Static balance	Small group, large group